THE Second Half PLAYBOOK

BUILDING YOUR GAME PLAN FOR A WINNING RETIREMENT

- ☑ Career Plan
- ☑ Financial Plan
- ☐ Second Half Game Plan

Ed McClellan

ILLUMINARE
PRESS

www.illuminarepress.com

ISBN: 979-8-9907067-0-5 (paperback)
ISBN: 979-8-9907067-2-9 (ebook)
ISBN: 979-8-9907067-1-2 (hardcover)

Library of Congress Control Number: 2024910815

Ordering Information:
Special discounts are available on quantity purchases by corporations, associations, and others. For details, contact www.illuminarepress.com

Publisher's Cataloging-in-Publication Data
Names: McClellan, Ed, 1960 - .
Title: The second half playbook : building your game
plan for a winning retirement / Ed McClellan.
Description: Chelsea, MI : Illuminare Press, 2024. | Includes illustrations.
| Summary: A guide to preparing psychologically and emotionally for retirement. Provides stories and directed activities to help pre-retirees build an exciting and fulfilling vision of their retirement years.
Identifiers: LCCN 2024910815 | ISBN 9798990706705 (hardback)
| ISBN 9798990706712 (pbk) | ISBN 9798990706729 (ebook)
Subjects: LCSH: Retirement – Planning – Handbooks and manuals.
| Retirement – Psychological aspects. | Retirement – Social aspects. |
Self-actualization (Psychology) in old age. | BISAC: PSYCHOLOGY /
Developmental / Adulthood & Aging. | FAMILY & RELATIONSHIPS /
Life Stages / Later Years. | SELF-HELP / Personal Growth / Happiness.
Classification: LCC HG1062.M33 2024 | DDC 646.79 M--dc23
LC record available at https://lccn.loc.gov/2024910815

"For the second half of life to be better than the first, you must make the choice to step outside of the safety of living on autopilot. You must wrestle with who you are, why you believe what you profess to believe about your life, and what you do to provide meaning and structure to your daily activities and relationships."

— **BOB P. BUFORD,**
HALFTIME: MOVING FROM SUCCESS TO SIGNIFICANCE

DEDICATION

To all our clients: Thanks for the lessons. You constantly show us that it is through deliberate, thoughtful planning that we create our lives.

Contents

Dear Reader,

This is all about YOU—you and your vision of life after career. My goal is to share insights and stories from my own experience in hopes of motivating and inspiring you in some small way. My fondest desire, however, is that you use the content, focus questions, guided activities, and journaling space in this book to purposefully create (and continuously grow and evolve) your personal game plan for a brilliant "Second Half." I want you to immediately broaden your ideas about retirement.

Long ago, "retirement" was celebrated as a *very special day* after a long career with a company to which you had loyally devoted many decades of service. They would throw a farewell luncheon with a nice cake, give you a watch (or some other token of appreciation), shake your hand, and wave goodbye as you went off to enjoy your "golden years."

While there are still folks who might spend 30 years or more with the same company, this model has become extremely rare. More and more working-aged people (with very high degrees of motivation, vision, and planning) curate their careers. People change employers or build new companies as their own needs, goals, and visions evolve. I encourage you, dear reader, to approach your Second Half of life with the same creative attitude with which people build their careers today.

If you have *any* vestige of the stodgy old image of retirement as a single day of celebration, throw it in the scrap heap now! Trash the idea of retirement as an event. Immediately replace the concept of "retirement" with *"creating your Second Half."* Just as people today methodically develop and grow their careers, you have the freedom to create the life you want after your career! The difference (and biggest advantage) is that in retirement (if you've properly planned and prepared) you have the luxury of making choices with almost no regard to their financial impact on your life. Ideally, in your Second Half, you won't have to choose a job primarily based on the salary and benefits. Even if you choose to work part-time, you should have the luxury of choosing a "fun job" primarily for the social or intellectual stimulation it might provide.

While 74% of the population has made a serious effort to plan financially for retirement, only about a third of those people have made a serious effort to plan psychologically or emotionally for retirement.[1] I think this number is *very* high. In all my years of service, I can tell you this with certainty: The number of people who have prepared for the psychological shift from "accumulation mode" to "distribution mode" is rare. There is a BIG mental change that must occur for you to be comfortable replacing a regular paycheck with distributions from a nest egg that you've spent a career building.

More importantly, to the point of this book, most people have a very hard time describing how they will spend their time when

---

[1] "2018 Retirement Confidence Survey," Employee Research Institute, April 24, 2018, https://www.ebri.org/docs/default-source/rcs/1_2018rcs_report_v5mgachecked.pdf?sfvrsn=e2e9302f_2

they retire. Good financial planners work very hard to encourage their clients to retire *to* something they LOVE, not *from* something they don't. Sometimes, it works. My experience, however, is that repeating this simple phrase is like giving a six-year-old a crayon and a big blank canvas. If you ask my granddaughter to draw her perfect day, she might draw a picture of the sun or Bonnie, her new dog. Another time, it could be a unicorn or a soccer ball.

On any given day, a client might describe his or her ideal retirement as playing more golf or spending more time with the grandkids. Lots of folks have given me similar one-sentence answers. After the first 30 days of retirement, they are bored to death. They are lost without a map.

Everyone understands that, when approaching retirement, you must be comfortable that you've saved and invested enough to support your income requirements for many, many years. The calculation of a shortfall in the actual amount of savings required is referred to as a "wealth gap." Once you and your financial planner are comfortable there is no wealth gap, I recommend that you devote just as much effort considering your **"self-actualization gap."** That is, after you retire, what is the gap between your ideal self and your current skills, interests, and abilities? *Who will you BE and what will you DO? Who will be in your circle of family and friends when you're not working full time and your only "job" is to live your Second Half in the most rewarding and fulfilling way for YOU?*

You've worked hard to get to this point in your life. This book is designed to help you envision and create a complete, three-dimensional picture of *your ideal retirement*. Used to its fullest, I hope that this guided journal will help you uncover and address your own self-actualization gap. While I also call it a "playbook," I won't torture the sports metaphor too far. The truth is that I chose this title because I completely reject the term "bucket list." I encourage you to strike this phrase from your vocabulary for two reasons.

The first reason that each of us should reject this term is its obvious association with the euphemism "kicking the bucket." While we're all mortal and we should (sometimes) make decisions acknowledging our own mortality, it is a negative connotation and completely counterproductive to *living your life in the here and now, enjoying every day to the fullest.*

Second, a bucket is something that you must carry. The heavier the bucket, the harder it is to carry. The term conjures an image of an old metal bucket with a thin wire handle that cuts into your hand. The result of this imagery is that we're inclined to put as little as possible into the bucket to make it as easy as possible to carry. On the contrary, *I want you to fill your bucket!* Think instead of a beautiful, all-inclusive buffet that is overflowing with every possible delicious, healthy choice of items from every corner of the world. Everything is laid out before you to taste and savor, reject, or enjoy.

Have you ever been to a buffet where there is some new exotic item that you've never tried? This is your opportunity to try new things! Take a bite! If you don't like it, don't eat it again! If it's something you find really pleasing, take another helping and take time to learn more about your discovery. In each section of your playbook, I encourage you to load up your own buffet by listing everything that you ever thought about trying. Make your master list one of abundance. Make it awesome as well as ambitious!

Take lots of time creating your Second Half through building your playbook. Fill it with things that are meaningful to you. You've spent a lifetime saving and investing financially for retirement. Invest the time and energy to prepare psychologically and emotionally. I'm going guide you by proposing some big categories, a few stories, and some idea starters so that you can start building your playbook for your Second Half. In the end, I encourage you to think of this book as your blank canvas on which you're going to draw up all your unique plays. Fill your playbook with things that are simple or grandiose, cheap, or expensive—make your playlist completely unique to you. The key is that whatever you put in your playbook should bring *you* joy and fulfillment. My effort will be to guide and motivate you to create the most expansive, most creative, and most unique playbook for playing and winning your Second Half, *however long it may be!*

This guided journal is divided into six unique parts so that you can organize your thoughts and plans. You will quickly discover that, just as all the parts of our lives can overlap and weave together in patterns strange, unusual, and beautiful, all the parts of your playbook can weave together in fascinating ways. New experiences or places could become motivation for yet more travel and more new experiences. Hobbies can help you create or maintain relationships with all your people. Difficult tasks that you love might require special equipment or ongoing learning/training and become yet another avenue for new hobbies and meeting new people.

So, dear reader, while I sincerely hope that you find some of what I share interesting and motivating, your time and energy creating *your* playbook is the important work before you. Take your time with the focus questions and guided exercises. Create *your* playbook by making great big master lists. Continuously revisit your master lists in each part. Add things, remove things. Continue the process of learning and growing throughout your entire Second Half. Make it a regular practice to choose items from your master list and add just a few things to your short lists every year. Don't wait! Start the process of creating your playbook today. Focus on winning your Second Half by creating your own plays!

Chapter One

NEW EXPERIENCES

*Every new experience brings its own
maturity and greater clarity of vision.*

— INDIRA GANDHI, FORMER PRIME MINISTER OF INDIA

My earliest exposure to working with a financial advisor involved sitting with my mom and dad while they reviewed their portfolio. Together with their financial planner, Ricardo, they reviewed their retirement goals and their budget, current assets, and investments. At a certain point in the conversation, Ricardo looked at Mom and Dad and asked them, in all sincerity, "Have you ever flown first class?"

That question had a deep impact on my parents. Dad was born in 1937, and his childhood memories of living through the Great Depression have had lasting impacts on his entire life.

When Dad was about to turn 12 years old, he asked his parents to buy him a pound of *real* butter (a rationed commodity) for his birthday. He said that he'd happily share it with the whole family.

In high school, Dad got a job at the local newspaper (*The Petoskey News Review*) and saved enough money to buy his family their first television. He also bought and paid for their very first car, which he shared with his father. After graduation from high school, my dad proposed, and my mother showed her father the very pretty but modest engagement ring. Her father's only words were, "You're going to wish to hell you could eat that thing someday."

My parents told me that they were both "raised broke," and it was through this lens that they worked hard and handled their finances. By necessity, they frugally budgeted and saved and invested their money. They had arrived at a point when they were about to retire, and their financial advisor had to shock them into recognizing what they had accomplished.

Of course, their answer to the question about flying first class was something like, "No way! We would never waste money like that!" To which their very astute advisor replied, "Well, if you don't start spending some of this money on yourselves, I guarantee that this young man next to you will be flying first class someday!" This certainly got their attention!

Mom never did fly first class before she died in 2008. Dad is still alive and very active at 87 years old, but he would still never waste good money on that kind of luxury. However, the point Ricardo made was well-received, and Mom and Dad did have many, many wonderful adventures together before her death at age 71. After some exploring, they chose Myrtle Beach in South Carolina as their late-winter getaway spot, renting a seaside condo for six weeks every spring. They were able to take a wonderful Caribbean cruise, treating my grandma and great-aunt to experiences they never dreamed possible. They also took the better part of one summer to drive Old Route 66 across the United States in a nostalgic journey to see a part of America that was disappearing all too quickly.

I've worked with many people from my parent's generation. In most cases, their default setting is frugality. No matter how much or how little they've saved for retirement, they consistently live well below their means. I think back often to that meeting with Ricardo and realize that an important part of my work is to drive home the fact that beyond a certain point, money does not buy happiness. If you've accumulated enough to replace your necessary and discretionary expenses in retirement, the very best thing you can do to fund your "happiness score" is to accumulate more and more experiences.

Whether it's touring the Kentucky Bourbon Trail or hiking part of the Appalachian Trail, there is only more joy to be had in going out and experiencing life. You could try to taste every variety of tea in the world and keep a journal. You could see every museum (large or small) in your state, or you could try to see a hockey game in all the National Hockey League stadiums in North America. The list is endless. The point here is that no matter the size of your budget or nest egg, nobody gets out of here alive, and nobody takes any money with them. With that as a given, experiences are all that matter.

Take time with the exercises and activities that follow to create your list of experiences to pursue in your Second Half. While I love to share stories, this playbook is all about YOU. If you don't create it for yourself, who will? Read through a few of my stories, which are intended to inspire and encourage you. But spend most of your time on the reflection questions, activities, and blank journaling pages to create your playbook.

Have fun! It's your life and your journey. You built a career over decades of trial and error. You made some choices that worked out well. You probably tried some things that didn't pan out the way you hoped, but hopefully, you learned something along the way. Your Second Half should be the same. In each part of this workbook, load up your lists of plays to try. Keep the things you love. Toss out the things you don't.

THE MEASURE OF YOUR YEARS

This exercise is intended to help you develop perspective regarding the size and scope of your own Second Half. How many years have you spent in the world of work—building a career, creating income, paying bills, saving money, and building a solid foundation for the opportunity to enjoy your Second Half?

<u>Equipment required:</u> A tape measure, a floor, a deep breath, and a dose of serenity.

<u>Actions:</u>

➤ Extend and lock the tape measure on the floor to 100 inches.

➤ Stand next to the inch number that corresponds to your current age, with zero to your left and 100 to your right.

➤ Look left at the number zero. Consider the age at which you started your work life. What portion of your life has been devoted to work?

➤ Look to your right to 100. Consider the average life expectancy for someone in similar health. Add 10%

(because you're better than average!).

Consider the growth of your mind, body, and spirit between birth and age 18. You have a proportional opportunity for growth between the ages of 60 and 78! Or 70 and 88! Or 80 and 98!

Consider the segment of your years spent preparing for and working in your career. What aspects did you love and want to include and expand on in your Second Half?

TRY EVERYTHING

Upon graduating from a very small middle school, both of my daughters attended a very large public high school in Ann Arbor, Michigan.

With more than 4,000 students, it was about the size of a community college, and it offered every conceivable type of athletic team, class, and club. It was overwhelming.

My advice to them was this: *Try everything* that you think you might be interested in, and by the time you enter your junior year, you should have a good idea of things you like, things you don't like, and things you love. Even then, I told them, you'll continue to add and weed things out as you learn and change, and eventually, you'll choose a college or career after high school. My advice to folks facing their retirement years today is the same as it was to my daughters back then. When it comes to experiences, try everything!

If you've always thought it would be fun to become a private pilot, find a local club or flight school to take you for a ride. In most cases, a one-hour discovery flight is $200 or less. You'll go up with a local, licensed pilot, take a tour around your local area, and get a feel for what it's really like. If you love it, you can add it to the short list of things that you might eventually turn into a permanent hobby. The worst-case scenario is that you have a new experience and find out it's not for you. (You'll also have a new cool story to share with family and friends!) Trying new things should be an ongoing process that occupies the entire Second Half of your life!

Everything starts with new experiences, and your playbook can tie them all together in the most beautiful way. I have a dear client who discovered a love of quilting years ago. In retirement, she found a local club to support this new hobby. Not only do the members get together to share quilting tips and tricks, but they also travel together to shows and conventions. They have fun together while they work to improve their craft.

This club has also found that their quilts bring comfort and joy to numerous families at C.S. Mott Children's Hospital at the University of Michigan. What started as a new hobby for my client became a beloved pastime. It has also helped her grow her list of **PEOPLE and CONNECTIONS** with whom she shares this entire experience. Further, it became an amazing gifting program and will contribute to a legacy, providing tokens of love to many, many families at the hospital during times of crisis.

Have fun on the following pages. List EVERYTHING you've always thought you might like to try. Big or small, it doesn't matter. Just like your retirement savings, your list of experiences should be something that you can't outlive. It should be an expansive and evolving list. You can refer to this list as often as you want. If you try something and don't like it, cross it off your list! If you love it, consider moving it to **CHAPTER FOUR: Lifelong Learning and Hobbies**.

FOCUS QUESTIONS

Read each question and respond. Some questions will be simple and your answers straightforward. Some will be more subjective and require more thoughtful consideration. Your answers will reflect who you are today, and they will change over time as you create (and recreate) your playbook. Revisit these questions from time to time. They should help you *start* your playbook. They should also help you later as you gain new information, knowledge, and experiences. Think about how your ideas change over time with every new experience.

1. How old are you today?

2. What mental and physical exercises can you do to make sure you're not "too old" for the experiences you still plan to have?

3. At what age did your parents or grandparents die?

4. What types of activities or experiences can you still do at age 90, 95, 100?

5. What types of activities should go on the front burner, while you are still young enough to do them?

6. What hobbies, interests, or activities did you love when you were younger?

7. What experiences do you want to have alone or with other people?

8. Do you know people in your community who enjoy similar activities or experiences?

9. What do you want to experience that is affordable for you—or even free?

10. What experiences do you want that may be expensive and require advance budgeting?

YOUR PLAYBOOK: EXPERIENCES

Master List

Master lists in each part of your playbook should include everything you can imagine. Over time, you can add to them, subtract from them, and check things off as you go. It should be a continuous source of new possibilities, big and small. You should never outlive your master lists. Whenever you're even a little bit bored, refer to your master lists for renewed inspiration!

EXPERIENCE	LOCAL CONTACT	EXPENSE (LOW, MEDIUM, HIGH)	ALONE OR WITH SOMEONE ELSE?
Scuba Diving	Dive Shop	$$	With Sarah
Welding Class	Comm. College	$	
Paint and Pour	Local Business	FREE LESSON	
Bonsai Class	Garden Club	$	With Bill, Joyce & Cindy

MAKING THE SHORT LIST

From your master list, prioritize a few things that are most important to you *today*. Multi-tasking is great for computers but bad for people. You can only do one thing at a time, so choose just a few things that you can do over the next year, for example. Then plan using your favorite calendar. (A blank calendar is provided below to help you visualize and organize your time.)

Top five experiences to try this year (from the master list above):

1.

2.

3.

4.

5.

Calendar and Planning

January

February

March

April

May

June

July

August

September

October

November

December

RECORDING YOUR WINS

Use the space below to post just a few pictures of yourself enjoying these new experiences. Most of us keep our photos on our phones or post them on various social media sites. These are great for sharing with others. This space, however, is specifically for YOU. Recording even a few of your activities in this space will reinforce and encourage you to keep the playbook process going throughout your entire Second Half. Enjoy reflecting, revisiting, AND BUILDING your playbook lists for all the years to come!w

Photo Gallery

PHOTO #1:

PICTURE OF YOURSELF IN ONE OF YOUR FAVORITE NEW EXPERIENCES OF THE YEAR.

Description: Names, Dates, People, Group, etc.

Photo Gallery

PHOTO #2:

PICTURE OF YOURSELF IN ONE OF YOUR FAVORITE NEW EXPERIENCES OF THE YEAR.

Description: Names, Dates, People, Group, etc.

Photo Gallery

PHOTO #3:

PICTURE OF YOURSELF IN ONE OF YOUR FAVORITE NEW EXPERIENCES OF THE YEAR.

Description: Names, Dates, People, Group, etc.

Note Pages

____

____

____

____

____

____

____

____

____

____

____

____

____

____

Every new experience can stimulate the desire for more. If you try something new that you enjoy, think about all the places you might go to deepen your exposure and involvement. Turn now to Chapter Two: Places to Visit!

PLACES TO VISIT

*Through travel I first became aware
of the outside world; it was through
travel that I found my own introspective
way into becoming a part of it.*

— EUDORA WELTY, WRITER, AND PHOTOGRAPHER

For most people, traveling plays a major role in their Second Half. Nothing opens your mind like visiting new places, near or far. You always see the world from a different perspective. However, no other category of your Second Half Playbook has as much potential to break a perfectly planned budget! So, while I want to share stories that will inspire you to organize and build your Playbook of Places to Visit, I also want to encourage you to create and maintain a systematic budgeting strategy for these expenses.

Depending on the destination and the level of accommodation you desire, costs can vary greatly. For budgeting purposes, it's important to acknowledge the potential range of costs for the items on your list. As much as possible, create an annual budget for discretionary travel within your regular, monthly spending. You can also create and maintain your list of PEAK EXPERIENCE travel destinations. These will probably be bigger expense items and might require a little more advanced budget planning!

Following one or two very good years of returns in your portfolio, you might consider taking some of your gains and booking one of the more expensive trips. On the flipside, while riding out a particularly bad stretch in the markets, you might consider checking off a couple of the close-to-home items on your list that can be funded from your regular, discretionary budget. Always keep a list of nearby places and attractions that involve less travel and expense but are *still completely enjoyable and fulfilling.*

Share your master list with your financial advisor when completing your annual reviews. This may be news to you, but your financial advisor hates it when you spring something on them that could easily have been planned for. The worst possible outcome for you is that your advisor must sell a perfectly good investment on a down market to pay for something that you knew you wanted but hadn't shared yet. The more your advisor knows about big, upcoming expenses, the better they can help you plan for the expense.

"Matching maturities" of your fixed income investments to the exact timing of a major, planned expense is a good strategy that might apply here. That is, if you know that you have a major purchase planned in five years, your advisor might find a CD or a bond that will mature at the same time.

Just as you planned together for your big goal of retirement, talk with your advisor about the big expense travel goals in your Playbook!

LESSON LEARNED: PLAYBOOKS ARE UNIQUE TO EVERYONE

A longtime client, whom I'll refer to as "Mel," told me that she'd been diagnosed with a terminal brain tumor. She said that she wanted to make sure that everything was in order. While taken aback by her matter-of-factness and saddened by her news, I took a deep breath and took my cues from her.

We discussed ways to "speed" up her playbook, since the end of her Second Half would come more quickly than she had expected. I urged her to talk about some of the places that she might want to visit. She had a boyfriend with whom she was close. She was also very close with her sister. I imagined that if I asked my own version of the "Have you ever flown first class?" question, she might decide to go somewhere exotic like Italy or Alaska with one of them and really live it up while she was physically able. I was surprised when she said, "I'd like to see the northern lights before I die."

One of the lessons I learned from this interaction is that I will never assume or project my own target travel destinations onto a friend or client. Just because I love Hawaii, Tuscany, and the South of France doesn't mean that that those places will be high on anyone else's list. YOUR list should be YOUR list.

FOCUS QUESTIONS

Read each question and respond. Some questions will be simple and the answers straightforward. Some will be more subjective and require thoughtful consideration. Your answers will reflect who you are today, and they will change over time as you create (and recreate) your playbook. Revisit these questions from time to time. They should help you *start* your playbook. They should also help you later, as you gain new information, knowledge, and experiences. How do your ideas change over time with every new place you visit?

1. Where have you already traveled?

2. What places have you visited in your town, county, or state?

3. What places have you LOVED? And why?

4. Do you enjoy adventure travel?

5. Do you prefer museums and historical sites?

6. How long can you sit on a beach or by a pool with a good book?

7. What vacation destinations, historical markers, theme parks, or points of interest are in your home (or neighboring) state that you've never seen?

8. What faraway destinations would you like to see before it may become more difficult to travel long distances?

9. Who are the people in your life with whom you would most enjoy specific travel experiences?

10. From what part of the world can you trace your family roots? (Exploring your genealogy and family history can develop into a fascinating hobby and provide an endless source of places to visit, people to meet, and interesting facts to share with everyone in your family!)

YOUR PLAYBOOK: Places to Visit

Master lists (in each part of your playbook) should include everything you can imagine. Over time, you can add to them, subtract from them, and check things off as you go. It should be a continuous source of new possibilities. You should never outlive your master lists. Whenever you're even a little bit bored, refer to your Playbook Master Lists for renewed inspiration!

Day Trips and Local Travel

We can spend a lifetime building a business or career and eating, sleeping, and raising families in our own little corner of the world. Yet, until we retire, we rarely have the combination of time, money, and/or energy to explore the cool places in our own backyards. When creating your playbook, take time to discover all the places close to your home that might be considered significant travel destinations for folks from other parts of the country. What is special and unique about your area?

Big cities everywhere have museums, churches, restaurants, sporting events, concerts, festivals, and tours of all kinds. If you're close to one, bookmark its calendar of activities on your web browser. If big cities aren't your thing, take some time to list all the nearby parks, waterfalls, national parks, nature preserves, lakes, rivers, hiking, biking, and camping areas.

Small towns everywhere also celebrate events of local significance. Embracing the change of seasons at a fall harvest festival can appeal to families and friends from all over. In this sense, "travel" can bring about deeper personal connections. Don't overlook day trips or easy overnight travel in your backyard, either.

With a list of places to visit within driving distance of your home, you should never, ever run out of things to do in any season. Take time to discover and travel locally!

MASTER LIST ONE: LOCAL TRAVEL

PLACES OF INTEREST NEAR ME	TRAVEL TIME	ACTIVITIES (WITH?)
Holland, MI	2 Hours (car)	Annual Tulip Festival
Lake Michigan State Parks	3 Hours (car)	Swimming with Grandkids
Detroit, MI	1 Hour (car)	Motown Museum, professional sports, annual boat show

Distant Travel Destinations

While short day/overnight trips can be spontaneous and easy adventures, travel to distant places requires more planning. Whether it's a signature golf trip or exploration of a new city or national park in another part of the country, we need to do more planning (and probably spend more money) in this category of adventures. The adage "he who chops his own firewood warms himself twice" applies here. In this regard, just the process of *planning* your travel adventure lets you "discover twice!"

Start with maps of the United States or the world. Look at your region of the country as well as distant locations you think you might want to explore. What ideas came to mind while reading through the focus questions? Just like your "Local Travel" list, don't limit yourself while creating this list. Continuously research, evaluate and prioritize your options. A successful, living list will grow and contract over time.

Through books, travel agents, or due diligence at the library or on the internet, you might cross something off your list that you added because of a preconceived idea of the place. On the other hand, you might discover somewhere that had never crossed your mind. As always, make this list your own. Don't be afraid to change it. Research and planning can be completely enjoyable and provide its own rewards as you learn about other places. "Warm yourself twice!"

MASTER LIST TWO: DESTINATION TRAVEL

PLACES OF INTEREST NEAR ME	TRAVEL TIME	EXPENSE	ACTIVITIES (WITH?)
Whistling Straights, WI	2 Hours (plane)	$$	Summer golf weekend with Rick, Mike & Dave
San Francisco, CA	4.5 Hours (plane)	$$$	Explore with Karen: Alcatraz, Fisherman's Wharf, Golden Gate Bridge

Peak Experience Travel
(Domestic or International)

In thinking about peak experience travel, we might be tempted to use that dreaded term "bucket list." I'm going to double-down on my insistence that you strike this term from your vocabulary, as it is completely detrimental to the positive thinking that should drive you in creating your peak experience list. When you check something off a bucket list, you're one step closer to "being done" (and checking out). Keep your list alive and growing.

Travel destinations that are truly our "peak experiences" should accelerate and expand our lives! Peak experience travel has the potential to give us memories and stories that last our entire Second Half. Moreover, the places we experience have the greatest potential to expand our horizons and widen our world view. The experience of these places gives us some of the most interesting tales to share with family and friends. They can also stimulate ideas for other destinations that we want to add to our master list for future research.

Seeing Scotland and playing golf there with my dad was indeed "a trip of a lifetime." Together, we made some great memories. More local (but just as significant for me) was a two-hour trip my wife and I made together to Kohler, Wisconsin. We stayed at a historic American inn, and I played golf on a beautiful course overlooking Lake Michigan where the Ryder Cup has been played. We also shot skeet and learned to fly fish. This was a "peak experience trip" for us within a very comfortable travel distance. There are peak experience travel destinations everywhere on the planet. Look far and wide AND close to home.

Your Peak Experience List of Places should continue to grow and evolve during your entire Second Half. It's not a list that should ever be marked "complete!" Take your time. Enjoy the process of creating, growing, and refining your list of peak experience travel!

MASTER LIST THREE: PEAK EXPERIENCE TRAVEL

PLACES OF INTEREST	TRAVEL TIME	EXPENSE	TRAVEL COMPANIONS/ TIME OF YEAR
Golf in Ireland	2 travel days + 5 days of golf + 2 tourist days	$$$$	*Mid-summer with Dad and friends*
Italy	2 travel days + 3 days in Venice + 4 days with Karen's family in Rome	$$$$	*Mix of tourist sites and spending quality time with Karen's Italian family*

MAKING THE SHORT LIST:
Local (or Longer) Travel

Top five PLACES TO VISIT (from YOUR master lists: LOCAL OR LONGER):

1.

2.

3.

4.

5.

Calendar and Planning

ASSIGN A FEW OF YOUR TARGETED DESTINATIONS TO ONE OR MORE OF THE PLACES ON YOUR MASTER LIST TO A MONTH IN THE COMING YEAR

January

February

March

April

May

June

July

August

September

October

November

December

Photo Gallery

PHOTO #1:

PICTURE OF YOURSELF IN ONE OF YOUR FAVORITE NEW PLACES OF THE YEAR

Description: Names, Dates, People, Group, etc.

Photo Gallery

PHOTO #2:

**PICTURE OF YOURSELF IN ONE OF YOUR FAVORITE
NEW DESTINATION TRAVEL PLACES OF THE YEAR**

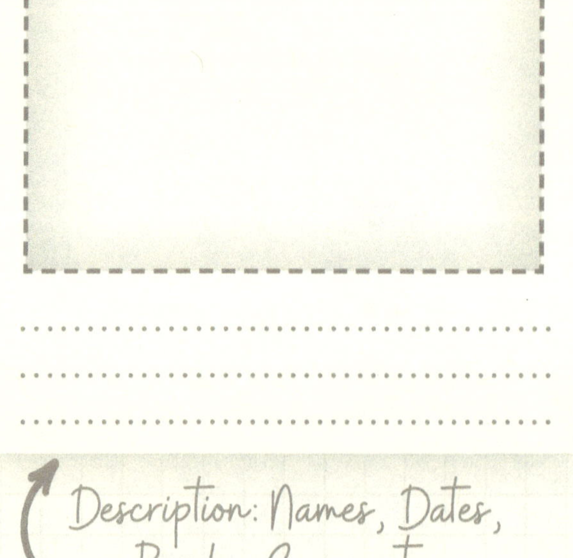

Description: Names, Dates,
People, Group, etc.

MAKING THE SHORT LIST:
A 10-YEAR PEAK EXPERIENCE
DESTINATION PLAN

Top five **PEAK EXPERIENCE PLACES TO VISIT** (from your master list):

1.

2.

3.

4.

5.

PLANNING YOUR PEAK EXPERIENCE TRAVEL

Share your list of Peak Experience Travel destinations with your financial advisor. Establish your budget and work together to set goals and realize as many of these items as you possibly can in the next 10 years!

RECORDING YOUR WINS

Maps are great as idea starters, but don't be afraid to go big in planning and recording all the places you see in your Second Half. For instance, my wife and I bought ourselves a very large map of the world. We used spray adhesive to mount it on foam board and bought a little box of multicolored map pins to identify places I've been, she's been, and we've been together.

Consider the focus questions and start your lists. Some companies specialize in making custom, high quality maps (along with color-coded push pins) that can double as attractive wall art and conversation pieces. These can help you record and document all your journeys and future destinations. (Check the "Resources" section at the end of this book for more information.)

Photo Gallery

PHOTO #1:

PICTURE OF YOURSELF IN ONE OF YOUR FAVORITE PEAK EXPERIENCE TRAVEL DESTINATIONS.

Description: Names, Dates, People, Group, etc.

Note Pages

Search Terms

Go to your favorite internet search engine and type any item of interest followed by the phrase "near me." Here are some idea starters:

National Parks, scenic highways, top wine producers, best golf courses, fly fishing rivers, best beach locations, states for hiking, waterfalls, cathedrals, best college football stadiums for atmosphere, natural history museums, car museums, music festivals, or boating lakes.

As you travel with family and friends, you'll undoubtedly meet new people. When you meet new, interesting people during your travels, put a little effort into collecting names, addresses, emails, and phone numbers. Ask for permission to connect through social media. Even if nothing else develops from the connection, it could be a simple opportunity to share photos of the places that you've both visited.

Shared travel experiences can be the basis for new connections and possibly more travel with new friends that share similar interests. Keep these new connections in mind as you turn to the next chapter, "My People, My Connections."

Chapter Three

MY PEOPLE, MY CONNECTIONS

Think back to the most important experiences of your life, the highest highs, the greatest victories, the most daunting obstacles overcome. How many happened to you alone? I bet there are very few. When you understand that being connected to others is one of life's greatest joys, you realize that life's best comes when you initiate and invest in solid relationships.

— JOHN C. MAXWELL, AUTHOR, SPEAKER, PASTOR, AND LEADERSHIP COACH

N eighborhood friends, high school buddies, college friends, colleagues from work—everyone has connections to people from all chapters of our lives. Whenever we leave ANY stage of life without a plan to stay in touch with people whom we care about, we inevitably lose our connections to those people, some of whom might have shared very important life events.

Years ago, I was invited to join a client friend on an annual golf outing the four days immediately after Labor Day. I joined him and his friends because I enjoy his company and I like to play golf. I had no idea of their history together. It turned out that the core of the group was made up of men in their 70s who had known each other since elementary school. They make plans to get together at least twice a year for golf outings in various spots in Michigan.

Their successful reunions over the decades are due primarily to the efforts of one man. Every year, Mike secures tee times at a golf course, books all the lodging and restaurant reservations, and plans golf pairings, games, and prizes for each day. Others step up and take on some responsibilities, volunteering to be a "condo captain" and collecting money from their respective groups. But Mike's dedication means this group has stayed in touch for more than half a century. They've shared births and deaths, illnesses, weddings, divorces, and funerals, and they truly care about one another.

I've only been a part of this group for five years, but I'm deeply moved when we gather in the evening around a small campfire for the day's "award" presentations and wrap up with a couple of guys playing guitars and leading the group in a sing-along of "You've Got a Friend In Me." (Even the classic, "Dead Skunk in The Middle of the Road" turns into a fun, bonding moment.)

When our youngest daughter graduated from her small eighth grade class, she and her friends planned to attend different high schools. At this moment of big life changes, the mother of one of her friends wanted to make certain that everyone stayed connected and started a book club for the moms. (Sometimes, I think it's more like a wine club with books.) This woman clearly saw that without a shared, purposeful connection, we would lose track of each other over the years as the girls' lives went in separate directions. Instead, we've shared many of our life events with these families. We've attended white elephant Christmas parties, weddings, births of grandchildren, retirements, and (very sadly) the funeral of one of the young women.

Make sure that you identify people from all chapters of your life who have shared in your greatest victories as well as your most daunting challenges. Those are some of the same people with whom you need to share your Second Half. Can YOU help be the critical lynchpin in at least one of your circles of friends? Do not fail to plan HOW you will stay connected with significant people in your life. Initiate and INVEST in solid relationships! Make certain that you have ALL YOUR PEOPLE to share life's infinite stream of joys, celebrations, and passages.

AS COUPLES RETIRE

I have worked with every kind of couple: straight couples, gay couples, mixed race couples, married couples, and unmarried couples. Once, I had a very dear couple in their late 80s confide in a hushed tone that they were "married in the eyes of God" due to a blessing ceremony with family in their retirement community chapel. They did not, however, choose to file a marriage license with the state. As this was a second marriage for both, they wanted to be certain that their individual estates were not commingled but passed to their respective children and grandchildren at their deaths. (Had I been involved with them earlier in their journey, I would have encouraged them to consult both an estate attorney and a CPA. I believe they could be legally married and accomplish their estate goals while also filing their taxes jointly. This might have saved them both a little money on taxes.)

Over many years, I've observed that one partner really gets into the numbers. That person loves to come to my office to complete the annual reviews, look over the portfolio, and talk about the market, the economy and yes, even discuss some politics. For the other person, reviews with their financial advisor where they are forced to talk about annualized rates of returns, interest rates, inflation—in fact, anything having to do with numbers, budgets, and economics—is on par with going to the dentist. This half of the couple is usually content to give their consent to any portfolio adjustments based on their partner's stamp of approval.

People are simply different. Acknowledging this is hugely important when approaching your retirement years. You may love someone for decades but only spend four to five waking hours with them every day. Then you're both retired and at home together 24/7. Even in the best of relationships, this sudden change can be jarring. You'll undergo a period of adjustment as you build your new routines.

Consider the case where a wife retires a few years before her husband. She establishes her daily routine, with her own balance of chores, leisure activities, and hobbies, and is living quite happily. When he retires, her established flow is completely disrupted with him underfoot every day. He has not yet discovered his own new routine and equilibrium. To her, he seems to get out of bed, shower, shave, and then look around the house somewhat lost as he begins to adjust to "life without purpose." This new "together time" can be a huge period of adjustment that needs to be acknowledged and prepared for.

I'm always honest when I can clearly see these two trains about to collide. I've asked bluntly, "Where you going to build your pole barn when you retire?" Of course, both people look at me a little puzzled before I add, "You two can't be together twenty-four/seven. You better have a plan to do some things separately." In most cases, the spouse who's about to retire becomes even more puzzled, but the spouse who has been home for a while now laughs and says something like, "That's right. I don't want you sitting around, watching TV, and messing up my routine!"

Every couple can (and should) enjoy many, many things together; however, they don't have to enjoy *everything* together. Make sure that you are prepared with a game plan to not only enjoy more time with your spouse but also to do things to stay connected to your circles of friends, even those that you might not share.

SINGLE RETIREES

My wife lost her father to cancer when she was just 14 years old. Her mother never remarried. My wife always said, "There is a special place in heaven for widows." I never really understood that until I watched my dad adjust to life without his wife of 51 years. Whether you find yourself living alone in retirement as the result of death, divorce, or by choice, it can take an extra effort to continuously stay engaged and involved with people in your social circles.

In so many ways, my dad is one of the biggest heroes of my life. After Mom died in 2008, my wife and daughters—and all our family—rallied and ensured that Dad was always included in every family event, even if it involved doing something he would not typically do.

One year, when a niece on my wife's side of the family selected a popular sushi restaurant to celebrate her birthday, we made sure that my dad was invited. My mom and dad had never, ever thought about eating raw fish, but Dad seemed to leap at the opportunity to give sushi a try. He ended up not liking sushi at all and never tried it again. But even so, since Mom's passing, Dad always says "yes" to everything, which keeps him engaged in life and his family.

Indeed, in a turn that I never saw coming, his relationships with his grandchildren have grown in quality and depth since my mother's death. He takes advantage of every opportunity to interact with every one of them.

For retired/retiring folks who find themselves single as the result of a divorce, the same principles apply. Staying engaged and saying "yes" to opportunities to try new things with family and friends is vitally important. Divorcées face special obstacles since they might have shared friends with whom they no longer have the same connections. It might be the source of modern comedy to ask, "Which friends did you get in the divorce settlement?" but it can be a source of potential isolation for one (or both) parties.

Despite the very real pain of being blindsided by unfaithful spouses and nasty divorces, many people grow and thrive on their own in unexpected ways. I have a very dear friend from high school who separated from her husband and became the lynchpin in gathering and organizing a small group of her friends to take a disco cruise together. She has done amazingly well at staying connected with lifelong friends.

Another friend who had previously delegated her financial life to her ex-husband took a lot of time with me to learn about her investments and has happily discovered that she is on a smooth financial path to a happy retirement. Not only is she going to be financially "okay" in retirement, we determined that she could also afford to buy a beautiful piece of land in the Upper Peninsula of Michigan on Lake Superior, where she intends to hike, fish, and kayak with friends, children, and grandchildren for many years to come!

A NOTE REGARDING LIFE INSURANCE IN DIVORCE

"Income replacement" is one of the most important reasons to purchase life insurance. Making certain that you have a plan to replace loss of household income from the primary bread-winner is important for every household. Life insurance can be like putting a new roof on your house. It's never going to be the sexiest purchase you make, but there is really nothing that can replace it for protection!

Divorce can be one of the most stressful life events a person ever goes through. I've seen many times where the stress is so great, a person wants to settle it as quickly as possible so that they can move on and start rebuilding a life that has been up-ended. In this time, especially if you are due to receive some regular income (alimony or child support) from an ex-spouse, make sure that income is protected in the event of that person's premature death.

In my professional opinion, every divorce decree should not only stipulate the amount of income to be paid and the time-line for these payments but also *how the payments would continue in the event of death.*

FAMILIES

As the saying goes, "You can choose your friends but not your family." It took me many years to realize that my grandpa didn't originate this. He was known for saying, "You can choose your friends. Your family, you're stuck with!" I'm sure he was not alone in this sentiment. Through luck or fate or karma, whatever your lens, everyone can relate to some degree.

Families can be our ultimate source of support, love, and encouragement. Sometimes, our families can also seem like a bottomless source of conflict, frustration, and exhaustion. We can be born into a family with which we feel no kinship at all. Or we can be born into a family that becomes the number one source of our support and identity. Likely, you have family members who cover this spectrum!

When we retire from the world of work, we ideally have more time to look around us and consider all our relationships with the luxury of more perspective and care. Take time and examine all your personal connections—*especially* those with family members—with more consideration, kindness, and love in your heart. If you have very close family members, make plans to spend more time with them, doing fun things and sharing more experiences, travel, entertainment, and hobbies. If you're estranged from a family member, maybe there will be opportunities for reconciliation and discovery. *If nothing else*, if you have family members with whom any hope of relationship healing is dead and gone, your goal can be to at least forgive them in your heart.

I'm not qualified (nor is it the purpose of this journal) to preach to anyone about the spiritual or religious context of the power of reconciliation and forgiveness. Even if you don't ascribe to a religious tradition, you may benefit from the health effects of forgiveness. Consider this 2021 finding from Harvard Medical School:

> Practicing forgiveness can have powerful health benefits. Observational studies, and even some randomized trials, suggest that forgiveness is associated with lower levels of depression, anxiety, and hostility; reduced substance abuse; higher self-esteem; and greater life satisfaction.[2]

As much as possible, it's generally advisable to be on good terms with all the people in your life, *especially* your family!

A NOTE TO MEN
(OR THE MEN IN YOUR LIFE)

Dr. Geofrey L. Grief, author of the 2009 book *Buddy System: Understanding Male Friendships*, highlights important differences in how men and women make friends. One of the big conclusions of his work was that "men 'tend' (because I am not speaking of all men or all women) to have shoulder-to-shoulder friendships and women face-to-face friendships."

In an effort to address the need for more shoulder-to-shoulder opportunities, initiatives are springing up around the world to create spaces for men to work on shared projects of interest. In a 2023 *Wall Street Journal* article, "How Men Make Friends: Hammering Pieces of Wood Together, Plus Power Tools," Clare Ansberry interviewed some regulars at a "Men's Shed," where men (and a few women) gather regularly to build park benches, desks, and bird

---

2   "The Power of Forgiveness," Harvard Health Publishing, February 12, 2021, https://www.health.harvard.edu/mind-and-mood/the-power-of-forgiveness.

feeders together. The Men's Shed movement started in Australia in the 1990s to combat loneliness among retired men. It has grown to more than 2,500 sheds in a dozen countries.[3]

In 2021, the Survey Center on American Life reported that only 21% of men said that they had received emotional support from a friend within the last week compared to 41% of women.[4] This seems to support the idea shared by Belgian film director and screenwriter Lukas Dhont that there is an "epidemic of loneliness."[5] While a deep dive into the sociological roots of this phenomenon are beyond the scope of my work here, we can all acknowledge that retirement is time in our lives where this problem can be further exacerbated through diminished social contacts with ex-coworkers.

If you resonate with the idea of making friends shoulder to shoulder, look around your community for projects of interest to you. If you can hold a paintbrush or swing a hammer, consider a stint as a volunteer for Habitat for Humanity. Many communities seek good people to contribute in ways that improve life for everyone. You might even make some new friends working "shoulder to shoulder."

If you have someone in your life whom you want to help find a new sense of purpose, consider helping them find

3   Clare Ansberry, "How Men Make Friends: Hammering Pieces of Wood Together, Plus Power Tools," *Wall Street Journal*, April 20, 2023, https://www.wsj.com/articles/men-friendship-sheds-tools-8b80a6de.

4   Daniel A. Cox, "The State of American Friendship: Change, Challenges, and Loss," Survey Center on American Life, June 8, 2021, https://www.americansurveycenter.org/research/the-state-of-american-friendship-change-challenges-and-loss/.

5   Kyle Turner, "While Filming *Close*, Director Lukas Dhont Found His Own Kind of Catharsis," *W Magazine*, January 30, 2023, https://www.wmagazine.com/culture/close-movie-director-lukas-dhont-interview.

shoulder-to-shoulder opportunities in your community, whether it's building birdhouses or volunteering for a charity with other people.

FOCUS QUESTIONS

Read each question and respond. Some questions will be simple, the answers straightforward. Some will be more subjective and require thoughtful consideration. Your answers will reflect who you are today, and they will change over time as you create (and recreate) your playbook. Revisit these questions from time to time. They should help you *start* your playbook. They can also help you later, as you gain new information, knowledge, and experiences. How have your ideas changed over time with every new encounter with all your people?

1. Who are the people from your professional life who have been important to you?

2. What shared activities could be a fun way to maintain those connections?

3. What opportunities do you have to meet new and interesting people in your community and/or in your new activities, travel, or hobbies?

4. Are there people from high school or college you've lost track of? How can you reconnect? Reunions or homecoming events? Social media?

5. Are there family members with whom you've lost contact over the years? How can you re-engage with them?

6. When was the last time you had an extended family reunion or get-together?

7. Who are the "super seniors" in your family who may want to participate more in family life?

8. Are some people unhealthy for the wellbeing and happiness of your Second Half?

9. Who can you forgive in your heart, so that you can move on and create a positive, productive life?

10. Fill in the blanks: "When I'm with _______________, I'm happy and I'm the best version of myself."

YOUR PLAYBOOK: PEOPLE AND CONNECTIONS

Master Lists in each part of your playbook should include everything. Over time, you can add to them, subtract from them, and check things off as you go. It should be a continuous source of new possibilities, big and small. You should never outlive your master lists. Whenever you're even a little bit bored, refer to your Playbook Master Lists for renewed inspiration!

Master List of Friends and Connections in Your Life

FRIEND(S) NAME	HOBBIES/ INTERESTS IN COMMON	CONNECTION WITH MY SPOUSE TOO?	CAN I BE A "LYNCHPIN"?
Mike and Shelly	Golf, boating, wine	**YES**	All of Us
Jerry	Music, cocktails	**YES**	Me

Master List of Family Relationships

MASTER LIST OF FAMILY RELATIONSHIPS			
FAMILY MEMBER NAME	**COMMON INTERESTS + ACTIVITIES**	**CONNECTION WITH MY SPOUSE TOO?**	**WHO IS THE "LYNCHPIN"?**
Dad, Tama, etc.	Golf, UM football, gardening	**YES**	*All of Us*
Katie/Joe, Elisa/Devin Eloise, Lawson Dom and Gia	Travel, good food and wine, grandkids' activities	**YES**	

SHORT LIST: CAN YOU
BE A LYNCHPIN?

List a few of your closest friends and friend groups. Consider your hobbies, vacation spots or mutual interests. If you aren't the lynchpin of a given circle, is there someone else who might be or could be?

1.

2.

3.

4.

5.

RECORDING YOUR WINS
WITH YOUR PEOPLE

I recently reconnected with a friend, Brian, with whom I had worked in our 30s. Over the last three decades, we've stayed in touch sporadically. Our careers went in different directions. He continues to work in the fresh produce industry and has grown his business to great success. We talk on the phone once a year *at the most*. Recently, we reconnected, and I was very proud to hear of the new growth trajectory of his company. Not only has it become a major brand within the industry, but he is doing amazing philanthropic work, devoting time, talent, and treasure to important causes, including autism research and fair trade for American farmers.

Recently, in the process of converting many hours of old

family videos to digital masters that my wife and I could easily share with our kids, I rediscovered one tape that featured videos from the time when Brian and I worked together. It includes a company Christmas dinner with spouses, organized office events like basketball and racquetball games, and travel to a big company training event in Springfield, Illinois, where Brian and I searched for the smallest statue we could find of Abraham Lincoln. We called it our "search for the littlest Lincoln." It was great fun and very silly. We recorded ourselves in funny poses with various statues of the former president. Of course, ultimately, we realized that the "littlest Lincoln" was to be found in our very own pockets—on an old penny.

In watching these recordings with Brian, we rekindled memories of events we had forgotten. We also remembered people with whom we were once very close, those have either drifted away or are no longer with us, and Brian and I bonded all over again. In turn, the memories seem to give us more perspective on our life journeys. We have more appreciation for what we have accomplished and overcome.

Obviously, technology has evolved dramatically. Everyone can take photos and videos and instantly share them with anyone in the world. "Memories" even pop up sporadically in our social media newsfeeds.

In considering your Family, Friends, and Connections, think about the tremendous opportunity we have today to "record our wins" in terms of shared time and experiences. Technology and social media sites have built a perfect infrastructure for memories that will last in perpetuity. Hopefully, as we do this, we capture moments that all of us can use to connect more with our friends and families for many, many years to come.

Often refer to your list of people as you consider the next section of your playbook. Who are the people in your life with similar interests? Whom do you want to invite to join you as you consider lifelong learning and hobbies?

Photo Gallery

PHOTO #1:
**PICTURE OF YOURSELF WITH FAMILY OR FRIENDS
ENJOYING NEW PLACES OR EXPERIENCES TOGETHER.**

Description: Names, Dates,
People, Group, etc.

Photo Gallery

PHOTO #2:

PICTURE OF YOURSELF WITH FAMILY OR FRIENDS ENJOYING NEW PLACES OR EXPERIENCES TOGETHER.

Description: Names, Dates, People, Group, etc.

Photo Gallery

PHOTO #3:

PICTURE OF YOURSELF WITH FAMILY OR FRIENDS ENJOYING NEW PLACES OR EXPERIENCES TOGETHER.

Description: Names, Dates, People, Group, etc.

Note Pages

Chapter Four

LIFELONG LEARNING AND HOBBIES

Anyone who stops learning is old, whether this happens at twenty or eighty. Anyone who keeps on learning…stays young. The greatest thing in life is to keep your mind young.

— HENRY FORD, AMERICAN INDUSTRIALIST
AND FOUNDER OF FORD MOTOR COMPANY

Your Second Half Playbook can include many opportunities for lifelong learning to stimulate your mind and body. Too many times, I've seen retirees who let their world shrink dramatically. You can recognize these people by the stories that you know all too well because they've told you the same ones so many times. If they're nice people, you will politely smile and nod. If they tend to be argumentative or otherwise unpleasant, you may start to avoid their company completely.

In contrast, people who continuously challenge themselves by developing new skills and abilities are more likely to be engaged and interested in all of life. They also tend to be more *interesting* to their friends and family.

The English poet and philosopher William Blake said, "Mechanical excellence is the only vehicle of genius."[6] The meaning of this quote is profound when you consider anything you might consider as a lifelong avocation or hobby. The human mind is the source of all inspiration. Every architectural wonder or hit song was first conceived in someone's mind. However, it is *only* through the disciplined practice and perfecting of *mechanical skills* that anything becomes a reality.

The modern version of William Blake's philosophy is the "10,000-Hour Rule" popularized by the author Malcolm Gladwell. His assertion is that the key to achieving true expertise in any endeavor is simply a matter of practicing, albeit the correct way, for at least 10,000 hours.[7] Many people have debated whether 10,000 hours of repetition or practice can guarantee that you become an expert in anything.[8]

Thankfully, for the purpose of your Second Half, *the only thing that is important is that you **LOVE the practice!*** With all due

---

[6] William Blake, *Complete Writings with Variant Readings* (Oxford: Oxford University Press, 1966), 453.

[7] Malcolm Gladwell, "Complexity and the Ten-Thousand-Hour Rule," *New York Times*, August 21, 2013, https://www.newyorker.com/sports/ sporting-scene/complexity-and-the-ten-thousand-hour-rule.

[8] David Bradley, "Why Gladwell's 10,000-Hour Rule is Wrong," BBC, November 13, 2012, https://www.bbc.com/future/article/20121114-gladwell s-10000-hour-rule-myth.

respect to both Blake and Gladwell, very few individuals end up recognized as "geniuses" or "experts" of anything. The most important thing for each of us to consider in choosing an avocation or hobby is, **"Do you love the practice of it?"**

VERA

When I was in my 30s, Vera, my neighbor for many years, was in her early 90s. She had a truly dramatic life: She and her husband survived and escaped Nazi Germany during World War II. She shared stories that would be unfathomable to most Americans today. She had heroic tales of being separated from her husband and then rescuing him by "selling herself" to Nazi soldiers. Her stories could easily be turned into an amazing book or movie, and she shared them with me as we got to know each other.

I saw Vera every morning as I backed out of my driveway on the way to work. Over time, I learned that Vera walked two miles every morning to the YMCA in downtown Ann Arbor so that she could swim a mile in the lap pool. She would then walk home. At first, she declined all my offers to drive her downtown, even though my office was on the same street as the Y. She said that she firmly believed in the "use it or lose it" philosophy. One winter day, when the streets and sidewalks were particularly icy, she accepted my offer of a ride only because I was going there anyway.

Over the course of the next year, in 10–15-minute increments, I learned about her past and her heroism. Vera showed me the tree under which her ex-husband's ashes were buried. I also heard about how she worked on the *New York Times* crossword puzzle every day. I got updates on the one-mile swim times that she tried to maintain (or beat) and how she enjoyed talking with her husband at his tree on the days that she'd walk to or from the YMCA.

She also let me know in no uncertain terms that superficial people were of no concern to her and that she had no time in her life for people of little substance or small mindedness. My wife and I were extremely flattered the day that Vera let us know that she had observed us in the yard, loving (and correcting) our children, and that she "approved" of our parenting skills.

There are very, very few of us that have the historic, life history stories that my friend Vera shared. However, ANY of us can choose to walk, swim, or do very difficult crossword puzzles and push our physical and mental limits in our Second Half. Vera lived to celebrate her 100th birthday. Her swim times slowed dramatically, and she needed a lot of help reading the crossword puzzle clues, but Vera stayed engaged, interested, and interesting to be around every day of her life!

LIFELONG LEARNING: SOURCES OF INSPIRATION

Books

Whether browsing libraries, bookstores, or your favorite online vendor, books have been the store of the entire world's knowledge for millennia. Whatever you might decide to research or study, most certainly find a book on the topic. Some folks take great pleasure in the tactile experience of holding, reading, highlighting, and dog-earing their library of books. Others like the ease and convenience of downloading books onto their favorite electronic device. Some folks are auditory learners and love listening to their books. Regardless of your reading format, fiction and non-fiction challenge and expand your mind.

In your Second Half, take a little time and look at your old bookshelves. Do you have a store of books that you read and loved years ago? Many times, like re-watching a favorite old movie, you can pull a classic off your bookshelf and discover something you either forgot or missed the first time. Take some time to read. Rediscovering a favorite book by the fireplace on a cold and rainy day is like a visit with an old friend.

Podcasts

Podcasts are essentially on-demand audio files, with more than 4.3 million available on every conceivable subject.[9] If you use an Apple device, chances are that you already have a podcast application installed. (Just search your phone or iPad.) If you use an Android device, you might have to download a free app to search for items of interest to you.

Statista.com reports that 79% of people ages 12 and older are aware of this new technology as a valuable content delivery method. If you haven't embraced this technology yet, take some time and explore it. Whatever you chose to research or study in your Second Half, there is undoubtedly someone creating valuable content on the subject that you can find via your favorite search engine.

The learning curve is usually very short, and the supply of content is constantly growing. Podcasts can be an inexhaustible source of research and new information about any topic that you think might be of interest to you. One great starting place (if you have enjoyed some of the stories I've shared here) is my author website, where you can find links to listen to a few "Second Half success" interviews.

____

[9]   Podcast Statistics & Trends in 2024," Podcastpage, January 5, 2024, https://podcastpage.io/podcast-statistics/.

Lectures and Classes

Adult learners, non-traditional students, returning adults, mature learners—they go by many names. The point is that almost every community recognizes a growing number of adults who have chosen to return to school later in life. Sometimes, adults with careers and families go back to school to complete a specific degree. However, many folks entering their Second Half are also interested in acquiring new skills or knowledge. Many times, classes and lectures are available on an "audit basis," without any testing, grading, or homework requirements.

Whether advancing your understanding of world history or learning how to use a welding torch, look around your community for opportunities to keep your mind flexible and active. Expand your knowledge base. You might have spent your entire work life in one particular discipline. Enjoy this opportunity to actively seek out and explore any new subjects of potential interest to you!

Clubs and Organizations

Clubs and organizations exist for any type of hobby or activity you can imagine. Civic clubs like Rotary International (www.rotary.org) promote "service above self" with 46,000+ local clubs consisting of more than 1.4 million members.[10] Religious organizations and social clubs encourage shared missions to serve others and/or develop social connections and interactions among members. Some clubs are organized simply around a hobby or interest.

Are you interested in sharing common goals of improving life for others or promoting civic and environmental welfare? Are you interested in meeting others with similar avocations and interests?

---

[10] "Who We Are," Rotary, accessed February 13, 2024, https://www.rotary.org/en/about-rotary.

Often, clubs and organizations can provide two equally important functions in your Second Half: They can provide opportunities to give of yourself to your community AND provide a chance to be socially active with people of all ages and backgrounds who share your passions.

Look into clubs and organizations in your community. Whether civic, faith-based, or centered on a shared hobby, clubs and organizations can be one of the most important outlets for your creative pursuits and fulfill the need for social interactions in your Second Half!

Hobbies

The perfect hobby is one in which the mere practice of it brings us great joy. It should (ideally) be something that requires ongoing skill development and "mechanical excellence" that is not easily acquired or maintained. It can continue to challenge and fulfill us our entire Second Half.

Maybe you took a guitar or piano lesson as a kid. Maybe you took an introductory scuba lesson on a tropical vacation. Whatever it is, hobbies offer an ever-growing opportunity for discovery and new frontiers for your body, mind, and spirit. Have you "mastered" a challenging song on the piano? How about trying your hand at something tougher? Maybe starting a Mozart sonata will be enough challenge for the next year! Have you obtained your recreational diver certification? Perhaps you'll consider going for the next level with an advanced class in wreck diving or underwater photography.

Common advice to young people about to embark on their professional lives is to find a career that offers the intersection of their passions and provides the greatest economic value. This is great advice to anyone at their stage of life. We must make money to support ourselves and our families so we learn to invest our time and energy into careers that we enjoy and that will produce the necessary income to not only cover our annual expenses but also to save and invest for our eventual retirement.

You've saved, planned, and invested for this time of your life! You have the absolute luxury of choosing your hobbies and avocations based *solely* on your passions. Of course, there will always be some constraints. While very few of us have the space and/or resources to purchase a Steinway grand piano, you can certainly find a suitable second-hand upright piano in good condition. (Sometimes for the low, low price of moving it yourself.) Whatever you choose for hobbies in your Second Half, enjoy the luxury of following your passions and enjoying the freedom to pursue them without any regard to the economic factors that face someone just entering the workforce!

Teachers, Coaches, and Critics

In anything we choose to do, there will always be greater and lesser practitioners. There will also always be truly exceptional people when it comes to delivering the information or skills necessary to reach higher levels. Tiger Woods has reportedly employed four different swing coaches since turning pro. Imagine being the best in the world at something and still working with a coach to continuously improve! Whatever you commit to in your Second Half, be humble and curious enough to seek out appropriate instruction and coaching.

In many fields, you are recognized and celebrated formally when you reach a higher level of achievement. The martial arts award different colored belts to students who progress. Once a black belt is achieved, it is further subdivided into degrees. In fact, 10th-degree black belts in karate are so rare that there are currently only an estimated 20–30 in the world.[11]

Similarly, many recreational sports recognize players by assigning ranks or levels. Pickleball, one of the fastest growing sports,[12] assigns sets of skills to levels 1.0 (beginner) through 6.0 (professional).[13] Players will occasionally rank themselves. Sometimes, a particular group or club will provide skills coaching and help assign formal ratings to make sure players of similar skill levels always play matches that are enjoyable and challenging. This way, players of similar status and skill levels can also learn and grow together in the sport. Take advantage of any opportunity to practice and learn with other people in the same hobby!

In addition to teachers and coaches, there will always be critics. As much as possible, *steel yourself to criticism* that could discourage your efforts. When choosing an activity, *choose teachers and coaches* who will help you grow and improve. Listening to those who are a level or two above us can be extremely valuable in helping us advance our acumen and skill set in any field.

---

[11] Jeff Bell, "Saanich Man to Receive 10th-Degree Black Belt in Karate, A Rare Honour," Times Colonist, January 18, 2022, https://www.timescolonist. com/local-news/saanich-man-to-receive-10th-degree-black-belt-in-karate-a-r are-honour-4967646.

[12] Brandon Mackie, "Pickleball Statistics - The Numbers Behind America's Fastest Growing Sport in 2023," Pickleheads, February 24, 2023, https:// www.pickleheads.com/blog/pickleball-statistics.

[13] "Definitions of Player Skill Ratings," USA Pickleball, accessed February 13, 2024, https://usapickleball.org/tournaments/tournament-player-ratings/ player-skill-rating-definitions/.

FOCUS QUESTIONS

Read each question and respond. Some questions will be simple, the answers straightforward. Some will be more subjective and require thoughtful consideration. Your answers will reflect who you are today, and they will change over time as you create (and recreate) your playbook. Revisit these questions from time to time. They should help you start your playbook. They should also help you later as you gain new information, knowledge, and experiences. How have your ideas changed over time with every new class, podcast, hobby tried, or book read?

1. What do you love to do?

2. Are there things you loved to do when you were younger that you'd like to try again?

3. What items from the "Experiences" section of this book have you enjoyed the most?

4. Are there books, magazines, podcasts, or websites that you can use to increase your "mechanical excellence?"

5. What equipment or materials do you need for this hobby?

6. Do you know someone who is an expert (or at least well ahead of your level) in this endeavor?

7. Where are the closest community colleges or adult learning centers near you?

8. What physical activities are most enjoyable to you?

9. What hobbies will continue to stimulate your mind and help maintain your mental flexibility?

10. What local groups or clubs can you find to help foster hobbies and shared interests?

Your Playbook: Lifelong Learning and Hobbies

MASTER LIST OF HOBBIES AND AVOCATIONS

Master Lists (in each part of your playbook) should include everything you can imagine. Over time, you can add to them, subtract from them, and check things off as you go. It should be a continuous source of new possibilities, big and small. You should never outlive your master lists. Whenever you're even a little bit bored, refer to your Playbook Master Lists for renewed inspiration!

HOBBY FOR LIFELONG LEARNING AND GROWTH	EQUIPMENT AND MECHANICAL SKILLS REQUIRED	LOCAL EXPERTS OR CLASSES	ALONE OR TOGETHER WITH SOMEONE ELSE
Play the piano	☑ Learning to read music, ☑ Buy a piano or find. ☑ Practice studio	Local College or H.S. Tutors	*By myself*
Triathlons	☑ Running shoes, ☑ Quality bike ☑ Swimsuits for cold water	Local running clubs, swim clubs, swim coach, bike shop	*With others from my gym*

Short List

SHORT LIST: _______________________________

List five potential hobbies you will LOVE to practice in the Second Half:

1.

2.

3.

4.

5.

CALENDAR AND PLANNING

CHOOSE ONE OR MORE MONTHS OF THE COMING YEAR TO TRY A EXPLORE A NEW HOBBY

January	February	March
April	May	June
July	August	September
October	November	December

RECORDING YOUR WINS

Photo Gallery

PHOTO #1:
PICTURE OF YOURSELF IN ONE OF YOUR FAVORITE NEW HOBBIES OF THE YEAR.

Description: Names, Dates, People, Group, etc.

Photo Gallery

PHOTO #2:

PICTURE OF YOURSELF IN ONE OF YOUR FAVORITE NEW HOBBIES OF THE YEAR.

Description: Names, Dates, People, Group, etc.

Photo Gallery

PHOTO #3:

PICTURE OF YOURSELF IN ONE OF YOUR FAVORITE NEW HOBBIES OF THE YEAR.

Description: Names, Dates, People, Group, etc.

Note Pages

____

____

____

____

____

____

____

____

____

____

____

____

____

Everything in your playbook, including lists from the previous sections, tells the world something about who you are. Where you choose to spend your time, what you do, and who you spend it with tells the world everything about what you value. Turn now to thinking about your personal messaging to the world. What is it that you want to be known for? What is your Legacy to People and the Planet?

Chapter Five

LEGACY TO PEOPLE AND THE PLANET

I believe that the time to start thinking about your legacy is not at the end but at the beginning, because as I said, that's when you're able to do something about it.

— MIKE MATHENY, FORMER BASEBALL MANAGER AND AUTHOR OF *THE MATHENY MANIFESTO*

A miserly old man stashed lots and lots of cash in a safe hidden in his closet. On his deathbed, he instructed his wife to put all his money in the casket and bury him with it. He died, and before his casket was closed and dropped six feet under at the gravesite, his widow slid an envelope under his clasped hands. At the reception after the service, the widow's best friend asked, "Did you really bury all that money with him?" His widow replied, "I believe it was my sacred duty to carry out my husband's wishes. I took all that cash to the bank and put it into my account. I wrote him a check for every dollar of it and put it in his hands!"

It's an old joke, but it's still true: Nobody takes any money with them to the grave. Some people focus on spending all their money before they die, and that's great. The only problem is that it's hard to plan for, unless you can tell your financial advisor the exact day you're going to die.

Other people are so intent on leaving the biggest fortune possible to their kids and grandkids that they sacrifice their own lifestyle to make certain they do. Both extremes are wrongheaded. No matter what you believe about life after death, everyone can agree that money is useful only on Earth. The things that money can do for you, your loved ones, and important causes here on earth are what matter.

Regardless of your financial position in retirement, you will grow in spirit (and the hearts of others) if you spend some time and energy contributing to the world. Whether your gifts are monetary in nature or donations of time and talent, everyone can take some time to consider the legacy they leave when they depart this world. What will you be remembered for?

Financial Legacies

There are four potential recipients of our nest eggs when we die (or get sick): loved ones, charities, nursing homes, and the IRS. If we come to terms with this reality, we'll get motivated to set things up correctly!

There are many, many ways to create trusts, annuities, or life insurance contracts that can produce lifetime income for you for as long as you live AND protect whatever is left for your family and/or charities. Talk with your trusted financial advisor and a good estate attorney to make certain that your (leftover) money goes to whom you want, the *way* that you want, and as far as possible, with very little tax obligation. ***At a bare minimum*, make it a practice to regularly review the beneficiaries on all your accounts.** The goal should be to avoid lengthy, costly probate processes, regardless of the size of your estate.

Trusts can be created with your estate attorney that can deal with multiple contingencies. They can include such items as "spendthrift provisions," if you want to be sure that Junior doesn't spend all his inheritance when he's too young to make good decisions. **Charitable Remainder Trusts** can be set up so you receive lifetime income from the *corpus* (principal amount) and your favorite church or charity receives the balance. **Charitable Lead Trusts** generate current income for your favorite charity and at your death; the corpus reverts to your estate.

An estate attorney with whom I work regularly told me, "I'd rather die without a will and trust than get sick without advance medical directives and a durable medical power of attorney."

Facing our own mortality can be an impactful spiritual or psychological exercise in itself, but having these things done *well in advance* will grant you a huge amount of freedom to focus on enjoying your Second Half to the fullest.

One day in April 2008, my mom was acting funny, and we went to the hospital for an evaluation. We thought she might be having a stroke. I'll always remember her looking at me as we walked from the parking lot and saying, "You're going to feel awfully damn silly when they tell us there's nothing wrong with me!" I asked her to humor me. Within 24 hours, Mom was in the ICU, unable to speak or do anything for herself in any way. Within that very short window, she had had a seizure and the doctors had discovered a deadly brain tumor. Our family was in shock.

I'll always remember the (amazing) staff of nurses who thanked my dad for providing copies of their estate documents, including a document legally authorizing him to act on her behalf. This very small thing was very, very important at that critical time!

Sometimes, the best thing you can do is to make certain that your spouse and/or children won't be overwhelmed financially, emotionally, or physically in taking care of you. To this end, you might consider different types of insurance products. Some can be structured to provide a combination of death benefit with a provision for accessing the death benefit tax-free while you're alive to cover a variety of costs associated with long-term care needs. I've seen these policies used to help people pay for services that helped them stay in their homes longer. The policy money doesn't always have to be spent on nursing care! Talk with your advisor about these types of policies to see if they might be right for you.

If you KNOW that you have more money than you'll spend on yourself in retirement, consider gifting strategies now, while you're still around to see your loved ones put this money to good use! If you have kids starting young families, you can help jump-start *their* financial lives with several types of gifts. You can also consider significantly frontloading college savings plans for grand-kids, though annual and lifetime gifting limits apply.

Case Study: Phil and Cindy

Phil and Cindy raised three children, all of whom are successfully launched and on their own. Two of them work very hard and pay their own bills but are still establishing themselves on their career paths. The third is a very happy stay-at-home mom of two active boys. She is happily married, and her husband is very successful in his career. Given Phil and Cindy's high degree of comfort with their current incomes (that far exceed both their required and discretionary spending needs), here's a few of the additional "legacy" choices they made:

> Annual Gifting

- o For their two single kids, Phil and Cindy gift part of their Required Minimum Distributions (RMDs) every year to fully fund their annual Roth IRA contributions.

- o To "keep things equal," Phil and Cindy add half of the annual Roth contribution limit to each of their grandsons' 529 college savings accounts.

> Celebration of Family Milestones: On Phil and Cindy's 50th wedding anniversary, they took the entire family on an Alaskan cruise. Memories made!

> Life Insurance to Protect and Grow the Financial Legacy: Phil and Cindy each applied for (and purchased) $250k of permanent life insurance with "extended care riders." In the event either of them cannot independently perform one of the "five activities of daily living" (bathing, dressing, transferring, toileting, eating) OR is diagnosed with a permanent cognitive impairment, *the entire $250k death benefit becomes accessible for their use (tax-free) while they're*

alive for anything for which they might need assistance.

➤ Survivorship (Second-to-Die) Policy: This policy will pay $750k to the estate at the passing of the second person. This policy is important to Phil and Cindy in that they hope it will cover any inheritance (death) taxes due when their estate is transferred to their children.

➤ Charitable Contributions: If additional money from RMDs is not earmarked for something specific, Phil and Cindy can make Qualified Charitable Contributions (QCDs) to their church or higher education fund. QCDs are distributions from a qualified account paid directly to a charity. They can be used to satisfy RMD amounts and are tax-free distributions, but they have certain restrictions. If you are charitably inclined **and** do not need your entire RMD amount, ask your financial advisor for more details. (If you are already giving to a church or charity, do it with qualified money. Don't do it with after-tax money. This is a potential tax and budget savings!)

Values and Non-Financial Legacies

You can find tons of opportunities to share of yourself and create *lasting legacies without money.* What is important in consideration of your "legacy" is making sure your loved ones and your communities know what is important to you. How will you communicate and pass along your values now?

You communicate your important values with your family and communities by simply sharing your time and attention with them. I can't tell you how much it means to my wife and me when our grandkids simply walk the garden with us and help pick tomatoes. Our time spent together and the conversations we have with them are magical. Just teaching them to fish or talking with them around a campfire is rewarding. We can only hope that these memories last for them and that they grow to understand and appreciate the value of shared time together with family.

I have clients who work very hard to fund extended family vacations to create plenty of memories now. Not only is this a valuable opportunity to share experiences, but it's also a way to pass along family values. In very important ways, at all stages of life, our families learn from us. Let them know now that you care about your shared lives together at least as much as any (potential) financial inheritance. Let your kids and grandkids know that's what it's all about! See to it that you are enjoying life with family and friends together.

Beyond vacations with kids and grandkids, consider getting your family members to volunteer together at a food bank or nursing home. There are unwanted dogs and cats in every shelter throughout the country. Volunteer to walk a dog or pet a cat. Take time to create your master list of important causes. Time and talent given freely to your community has multiplier effects. You get back more than you give. That's the nature of service. Make sure that people know you by your works! What is important to you? What important values do you want to pass to the next generation and live beyond your individual lifespan?

Lifetime Achievement Awards

Have you ever been to an event or watched an award show like the Academy Awards, where they present lifetime achievement awards? These are awards that are always given to someone who has exhibited a long, dedicated history of service to a particular field or endeavor. It can be as grand as the Nobel Peace Prize or as humble as a Volunteer of the Year award from a local animal shelter, food pantry, or hospice.

Picture yourself at an awards banquet in your community. You are receiving a "lifetime achievement award for service to _______________." (You fill in the blank!) What do you care about? What service do you give to your community? What are you known for supporting? Legacies are not all about the money we leave. Some of the very best legacies to our families and communities are created through the time, attention, and service we offer, *especially in our Second Half!*

FOCUS QUESTIONS

Read each question and respond. Some questions will be simple and the answers straightforward. Some will be more subjective and require thoughtful consideration. Your answers will reflect who you are today, and they will change over time as you create (and recreate) your playbook. Revisit these questions from time to time. They should help you start your playbook. They should also help you later as you gain new information, knowledge, and experiences. How have your ideas changed over time with every gift given, talent or value shared, or volunteer hour donated?

1. Who are the people you want to receive your financial and physical assets when you're gone? (Do you have up-to-date beneficiaries on all your accounts and insurance policies?)

2. Is it a priority (or a necessity) that you spend all your money on your needs?

3. Who would take care of you if you were in need physically? Financially?

4. Do you have more than enough savings and income for all of your future needs?

5. What values are important to pass on (with or without) your money?

6. Which charitable organizations or causes do you really care about?

7. What are the current and projected future tax obligations on your assets?

8. Are there giving strategies that could reduce your overall tax obligation?

9. If you were to write your memoirs, what are the most important lessons learned that you would want to share with your family?

10. How will you demonstrate your most important values to your friends, family, and community while you live your Second Half?

Your Playbook: Legacy to People and Planet

MASTER LIST OF PEOPLE AND CAUSES IMPORTANT TO YOU

Master Lists (in each part of your playbook) should include everything you can imagine. Over time, you can add to them, subtract from them, and check things off as you go. It should be a continuous source of new possibilities, big and small. You should never outlive your master lists. Whenever you're even a little bit bored, refer to your Playbook Master Lists for renewed inspiration!

LEGACY TO	FAMILY	TIME, TALENT, OR TREASURE? GIFTING?	PASSING ON FAMILY VALUES
Kids	Katie and Elisa	All the above	*Very important*
Grandkids	Eloise, Dominic, Gianna and Lawson	UTMAs and 529 accounts	*Shared experiences and family vacations*

Short List

SHORT LIST: _______________________________________

List five things to do or talk about with your family, financial advisor, or estate attorney:

1.

2.

3.

4.

5.

Photo Gallery

PHOTO #1:
**PICTURE OF YOURSELF VOLUNTEERING
IN YOUR COMMUNITY.**

Description: Names, Dates, People, Group, etc.

Photo Gallery

PHOTO #2:
PICTURE OF YOURSELF VOLUNTEERING IN YOUR COMMUNITY.

Description: Names, Dates, People, Group, etc.

Photo Gallery

PHOTO #3:

PICTURE OF YOURSELF VOLUNTEERING IN YOUR COMMUNITY.

Description: Names, Dates, People, Group, etc.

Note Pages

Important contacts:

➢ Estate Attorney: _______________________

➢ Financial Advisor: _______________________

➢ CPA: _______________________

The topic of estate planning, taxation, and gifting is wide-ranging, ever-changing, and beyond the scope of this book. The key is to make sure you share your desires with both your financial advisor and your attorney. Make your lists and talk with your professional team about your goals!

With your awesome Second Half Playbook in hand, you might wonder how you'll have time for everything that you'd like to see, do, study, and accomplish. Turn your attention now to "Quitting Things You Hate" and find ways to make more time in your life for things that bring you more and more joy in your Second Half!

Chapter Six

QUITTING THINGS YOU HATE

*The difference between successful people
and really successful people is that really
successful people say no to almost everything.*

— WARREN BUFFETT, AMERICAN BUSINESSMAN,
INVESTOR, AND PHILANTHROPIST

Once you've invested the time and energy to create lists of all the incredible places to visit and experiences to have in your Second Half, you may start to wonder how you ever found time to work at all. I've had many happily retired clients over the years express this sentiment. So, how do you make time for all the things that you've listed for yourself in your playbook?

In Tim McGraw's song "Live Like You Were Dying," he sings about all the amazing things someone might do if they received a terminal diagnosis. The refrain mentions skydiving, mountain climbing, and bull riding, which are just some of the crazy, fun, exhilarating hobbies and activities one might choose! Until this part of this book, I've encouraged you to think about and create your lists with a little of this perspective, acknowledging your mortality while constantly thinking ahead, planning, and creating your Second Half. The flipside is that we should also put serious consideration into the time we spend in our Second Half on chores, duties, and obligations that really bring us no joy whatsoever.

What are some of the things you don't love to do? Large or small, are there things that you could delegate or hire to have done around the house? Are there things that don't really need to be done at all? If today was your last day on Earth, would you spend it cutting the grass or cleaning the bathroom?

We must complete many day-to-day tasks to maintain ourselves and our homes. Not every one of these regular chores can bring us joy, let alone be considered a "peak experience" for our Second Half playbooks. Still, these things—dishes, laundry, bed-making, vacuuming, yard work, bill paying—need to be done. It can seem like an endless, tedious list at times. How do we organize our thinking about these things? And how do we organize and prioritize our lives such that we are spending *more* time doing the things we love AND *less* time doing things we don't?

In business, it's obvious that putting the right people in the right jobs is a key to success. A good CEO should not attempt to do all things or be all things in a company. In my own career as a financial advisor, I understand it's necessary to consider tax law as part of every financial plan. That said, I personally hate doing the job of a CPA.

I love to build beautifully balanced portfolios. I love to read and digest economic forecasts and delve into P/E ratios and growth projections for individual companies. I'm one of those nerds who enjoy reading the fine-print prospectuses delivered by mail to investors.

On the other hand, I always hire a professional to do my personal and business taxes. While I certainly have the capacity to read carefully and plod through all the instructions that the IRS puts out every year on how to complete every form and schedule, I just hate it. I will always pay a professional to complete this important work that brings no joy to me.

We should think about all the tasks in our personal lives the same way a good CEO organizes all the activities of running a successful business. When my wife and I moved to a three-acre lot in the country, I decided that life was too short to spend cutting my own grass. I never cut my own grass anymore. You might love cutting grass. Great, cut your grass!

I do enjoy creative yard projects. I like growing watermelons, tomatoes, and pumpkins. I also like some landscaping projects that I consider creative outlets. Could I outsource much of that work, too? Yes, but I keep the things I enjoy and pay others to do the rest.

Before the idea for this book had even occurred to me, I asked my wife to write a list of all the things that she would do with her time once she gave up the job that she loved. She came up with tons of hobbies and activities that she was super-excited about. Cleaning the house regularly was not on her list.

As my wife had a better-than-average relationship with her

financial advisor, it was agreed that she could afford to retire AND hire a housecleaner every other week. With this modest budget adjustment, my wife freed up approximately eight hours per month to invest in all the cool things in her own playbook. Moreover, these hours are spent doing things that bring her happiness, not on activities that don't!

THE JOY/EASE MATRIX

To help organize your thinking about things you might choose to quit, I suggest breaking up projects into all their components. Some will bring you great joy; others will not. Some tasks you will find incredibly easy while others may be difficult, dangerous, or require special equipment. By listing and plotting all the tasks associated with any area of our life, we easily categorize all tasks into one of four zones:

A. "Like Little Pieces of Candy" Zone

B. Outsourcing Zone

C. Potential Hobby Zone

D. Growth Opportunity Zone

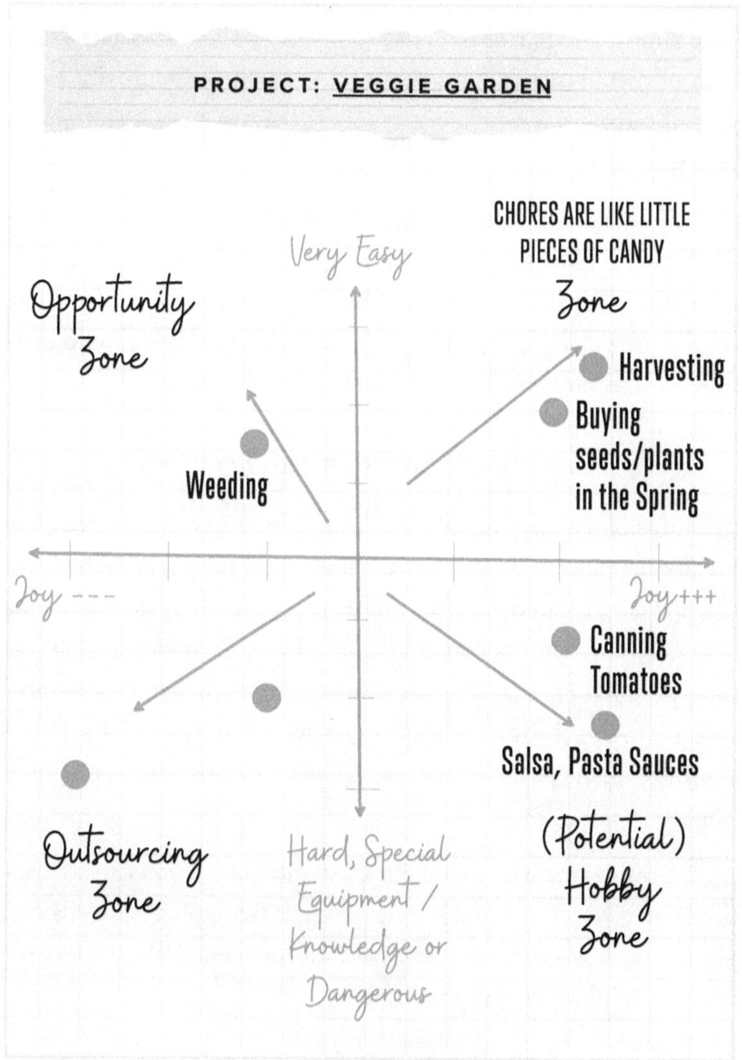

PROJECT: VEGGIE GARDEN
Very Easy
CHORES ARE LIKE LITTLE PIECES OF CANDY Zone
Opportunity Zone
Harvesting
Buying seeds/plants in the Spring
Weeding
Joy - - -
Joy +++
Canning Tomatoes
Salsa, Pasta Sauces
Outsourcing Zone
Hard, Special Equipment / Knowledge or Dangerous
(Potential) Hobby Zone

In the example below, I've plotted out tasks associated with having a vegetable garden. The various dots are plotted on two scales: "Joy" and "Ease." Of course, this is an example. You will have your own view of the relative joy or easiness associated with each of these tasks. What is important to think about with every part of our lives is where the tasks fall within each quadrant for you personally?

If you take the time to list out all the tasks associated with ANY part of your life, you can assign each a rating on your personal Joy/Ease scales. From there, it's possible to see where you want to focus your time and attention and where you should consider outsourcing or giving up different components.

"Like Little Pieces of Candy" Zone

My brother-in-law is an M.D. with a very busy family practice. He doesn't have a lot of time for home repair projects, but he loves them! He once told me that he keeps an ongoing list of repair and maintenance projects and treats himself by doing them as time permits. He said that it's like having "little pieces of candy" spread around the house, and he gets to pull out his tool belt and complete small projects when he wants to really relax and enjoy himself.

In my example charting out gardening tasks, you can see that the "Little Pieces of Candy" Zone includes shopping for seeds and plants and harvesting the "fruits of all the labor." These tasks for me are joyful, free-time activities.

Outsourcing Zone

In this zone, the combination of difficulty (danger or special equipment required) together with the fact that these tasks take *joy away*, make certain tasks prime candidates for outsourcing. Once you've clearly identified jobs in this zone, your biggest job is finding the right people to hire for the work. To use my gardening example, although you might enjoy researching and designing a beautiful fence for your vegetable garden, the physical requirements of digging and setting posts might be just too much. Create a budget, then search and find the right contractor for the job!

Potential Hobby Zone

When you derive great joy from tasks that are also difficult (or require special knowledge, skills, and/or equipment), you can consider these prime candidates for a Second Half hobby. In this example, canning tomatoes for use throughout the winter might bring a lot of satisfaction. The products of your labor will be enjoyed when you pull a jar of your garden-fresh tomatoes for use in your favorite soup or chili recipe in the middle of January.

You may note that you derive even more joy creating sauces and salsas with the vegetables from your garden. You might find you can make even more family-favorite recipes by using peppers, onions, and herbs. A person fully engaged at the ends of their own Joy/Ease scale produces something that can give them great satisfaction in both the creation AND the sharing of what they create.

Growth Opportunity Zone

The tasks in this zone require a little sorting out and extra consideration but (almost always) can provide us opportunities for growth and/or sharing with others. If the task is relatively easy but somewhat joyless, we have a couple of choices regarding how we approach the task. We can try to reframe the way we think about the task to make it less objectionable. We could also negotiate with a partner or friend for some sort of fair exchange or sharing of tasks.

Take my example of weeding the garden. While it may not be a particularly joyful task, it is relatively easy. It is also a vital activity to provide plants with the room to receive all the water, nutrients, and sunshine required for maximum production.

Faced with Opportunity Zone activities like this, we can attempt to negotiate with ourselves. We can try to alter our own thinking about the task, recognizing the huge importance that it plays in the overall success of our goals. We can try to think about the task as meditative and how happy we are with the end product: a weed-free environment for our beloved plants. We might even end up with a new appreciation for weeding!

An alternate approach is to collaborate with a spouse, partner, or friend on a project. Maybe you don't like weeding, but your partner or neighbor does. Moreover, the neighbor who planted sweet corn might jump at the opportunity to do a little weeding in exchange for some homegrown tomatoes or a jar of salsa at harvest time!

FOCUS QUESTIONS

Read each question and respond. Some questions will be simple and the answers straightforward. Some will be more subjective and require thoughtful consideration. Your answers will reflect who you are today, and they will change over time as you create (and recreate) your playbook. Revisit these questions from time to time. They should help you start your playbook. They should also help you later as you gain new information, knowledge, and experiences. How have your

ideas changed over time with every unpleasant, difficult, or dangerous task delegated to somebody else?

1.   What tasks do you do every month that you really dislike?

2.   What are some things you enjoy that can be done at any age?

3.   What are some things you could delegate if you live into your 80s or 90s?

4.   Fill in the blanks: "I would gladly do a little more ______________ if someone else would just do ______________ for me!"

5.   If you had the money, you would immediately hire someone to ______________.

6.   Which local companies specialize in providing the services that you find dangerous or monotonous?

7.   By saying "no" to some of these things, how much time will you free up to devote to projects, things, and people you love?

8.   Are there people in your circle (friends/family) who might like to help with some of your "weeding?"

9.   Life is too short to ______________.

10. Have you made commitments to groups, clubs, or organizations in the past that you'd happily let go of now?

YOUR PLAYBOOK: QUITTING THINGS YOU HATE

Master Lists (in each part of your playbook) should include everything you can imagine. Over time, you can add to them, subtract from them, and check things off as you go. It should

be a continuous source of new possibilities, big and small. You should never outlive your master lists. Whenever you're even a little bit bored, refer to your Playbook Master Lists for renewed inspiration!

Create a Joy/Ease Matrix for Anything and Everything

In this section, you'll find a few big category suggestions. Create a Joy/Ease matrix for anything and everything in your life. Make lots of copies and map out the tasks associated with any area of your life in which you'd like to create more space for joyful activities (while reassigning the unpleasant ones). The goal is to spend more and more time on things you love to do and less time on those you don't! You can download and print out PDF copies of the Joy/Ease matrix and many other blank copies of all the lists in this book for your use at illuminarepress.com.

Categories and Tasks

Maintaining a home

- Bills, budget, investments

- Regular cleaning

- Cooking meals, washing dishes

- Vacuuming, laundry, bathroom cleaning

- Grocery shopping

- Routine auto maintenance (including oil change)

Yard work

- Grass cutting, edging, hedge trimming

- Weeding

- Flower gardens

- Vegetable gardens

Community Service

- Church services

- Volunteer work

Travel Planning

- Research locations

- Maps

- Itineraries

- Reservations

Home Maintenance Tasks

- Painting, caulking, and sealing

- Furnace/AC filter replacement

- Water heater, regular draining, testing

Remodeling/Updating

- Research

- Design plans

- Cabinet shopping

- Appliance shopping

- Installation

Short List

SHORT LIST: ____

List five tasks to start delegating or outsourcing (include cost estimates for budgeting purposes):

1.

2.

3.

4.

5.

Note Pages

In Parting, Dear Reader,

If I've done my job, you've already started to flesh out parts of this journal. You've at least *started* to build a playbook for winning your Second Half. I hope you refer to all the lists, maps, and calendars that you've started for yourself. I also hope that you expand, change, and grow your lists often. Add to them, subtract from them, and continuously learn and grow from them. Your playbook should be full of everything you can think of that could bring you joy and fulfillment in your entire Second Half. You are the master of how your playbook develops over time!

Keep your playbook handy for your reference. Whenever you feel a little stuck, reach back into any part of this book to reacquaint yourself with your vision and take time to re-focus. Return frequently to the focus questions in any part of your playbook. How have your answers to these questions changed with each new adventure of your Second Half?

This playbook is yours. Share whatever you might have learned with others but always hold fast to your vision. Encourage your friends and family to start working on their own playbooks. By sharing what you've learned, you can help others on a similar journey. Imagine a world where everyone in your circle is actively engaged in creating and developing playbooks to win their Second

Half, striving to stay interested and interesting throughout the rest of their lives!

Creating your Second Half Playbook is an evolving journey. You didn't map out every move of your career on graduation day. You took time to make decisions and grew up along the way. Likewise, nobody knows with certainty everything what is going to happen to them during their Second Half. There are inevitable detours and course corrections along every journey.

Take time creating your playbook and revisit it often. Just because you have a "retirement date" doesn't mean you have to have your Second Half entirely planned out. You have the luxury of creating your Second Half any way you choose. Use all the knowledge and experience you've accumulated in your First Half to inform your playbook in your Second Half!

When it comes to playbook experiences, try everything. Best case is that you find something new that you love, and it becomes a bigger part of your life. Worst case is that you tried something that you've always wanted to try, and you have gained a great story!

In the same manner, always keep an ongoing list of places near and far to explore. Expand your mind by learning about different parts of the world. Short day trips can be just as exciting and fulfilling as longer trips. Peak experience trips require more research, planning, and budgeting. They can also be satisfying in two ways: First, as you research and plan, and then again as you travel. Wherever you go will impact you and provide you with interesting memories and stories to share with family and friends.

Be intentional about staying connected to family and friends who have shared the greatest victories and challenges of your First Half. These are the people who support and understand you. They helped form who you are. Invest time and energy maintaining solid relationships in your Second Half. Spend more time with all the supportive, positive people in your life.

Lifelong learning and hobbies can keep you interested (and interesting) in your entire Second Half. Look for the intersection of your passion and activities that require more skills or practice to master. When you find things in this zone, they can make for a bottomless source of satisfaction and joy.

While you shouldn't occupy yourself with thoughts of "kicking the bucket" someday, acknowledging that life ends can inform your decision-making process, especially when it comes to your legacy. Where and how do you want your (leftover) money to be distributed? What non-financial legacy do you want to leave? What values do you want to live beyond you?

Last, make time for all the joyful things in your life by quitting things you hate. Once you've done the work and created awesome lists of things to do, places to see, and memories to share with people whom you love, make sure you free up all the time you can for the great plays in your playbook!

Retirement is not a single day in your life. It's a journey. You likely built your career or business over the course of decades. Your Second Half should be no different. Work on your Second Half Playbook as purposefully and as joyfully as possible. I wish you all the best for a brilliant Second Half! Happy Retirement!

I'd love to hear about your success stories and lessons learned from using this journal. Please go to my website, illuminarepress. com, to share your experiences and check back often for continued inspiration. I'll frequently add more stories and interviews with friends and clients. Through listening and sharing with each other, we will make everyone's playbooks stronger!

"Just one thing a day."

One of my very happily retired clients told me that when she first retired, she stressed a lot when it came to thoughts of cleaning out closets and boxes and files that had been stored for years and years. She said that she always thought that when she retired, she'd finally get to all the "stuff" that had piled up. She envisioned living in a clean, well-organized, and de-cluttered house. Then one day she told me that it dawned on her that "slow and steady wins the race." She didn't have to get it all done that spring or that summer—or even that year!

"It took a lifetime to accumulate all this stuff, why am I pressuring myself to get it all cleaned out this month?!" she said.

Now she tries to do just one little thing from that list every day. If she cleans out just one drawer, one file folder, or one box before (or after) valued time with her grandkids, it's a big win. Her grandson will never think back about his time with her that day and remember clean closets. Nope. But he will remember his grandmother pushing him on the swing or picking fresh tomatoes together in her garden.

Acknowledgments

The term "acknowledgment" has two common definitions. The usual meaning in this context is to name and thank everyone who helped me on my journey of creating this book. I'll get to that. However, I'd like to begin by using an alternate definition: "acceptance of the truth or existence of something."

My truth is that I'm in the boat with you. On the cusp of my 64th birthday, I'm starting to freak out a bit when I think about retirement. What's next for me? If I'm not a Certified Financial Planning (CFP) professional, serving other people, a key person in their planning journey, who will I be? What will I do?

I acknowledge that I began to write this book as self-reflection and therapy. While I've learned a lot about what to do (and what not to do) by observing and coaching clients to retirement, I realized that it's an academic exercise until you face your own halftime. It may not really be my halftime. But, as you know by now, I'm a glass half-full person who prefers to use the term "playbook" versus "bucket list."

Writing this book has had a huge impact on me personally. I've assigned homework to my clients, such as starting lists of experiences, but organizing my thoughts in this format helped me know that I'm not personally ready to make that leap and retire—at least not in the sense of "one day you're working, next day you're not." I'll use these lessons myself for years to come as I build my own vision and playbook. I hope every reader finds as much value here as I have.

Moving on to proper acknowledgments, I would like to thank my beautiful wife, Karen. When I meditate on who you are, I always think of the song "Love Has Come" by Matt Maher. Nobody has taught me more about truly loving and caring for others than you have. You are an amazing, wife, mother, and "Nona" to our grandchildren. Your strength and energy in "retiring to the service of your family" is an inspiration.

Thank you for giving me so much extra space at home and on vacations while I worked on this book. For more than 40 years, I have appreciated your ongoing support and encouragement. Thank you for understanding the introverted dreamer who talked you into marrying him. Thank you for the space to quietly write.

Last, I'd like to thank Julie "the book" Broad and the associates at Book Launchers. You've all proven extremely professional and completely invaluable to a new author! As a self-published author, I could have hired anyone to just print and ship this little book. But I cannot imagine that I would have made it to the finish line (let alone produce something that I could be proud of) without your organization, continual support, and encouragement. Your team helped me transform a bare outline into a manuscript. I look forward to more lessons and work to come as you help me promote this book wherever it will help the most people. I look forward to a long relationship with the entire team of professionals at Book Launchers. Thank you all.

Appendices

APPENDIX A: Professional Designations and Their Meanings

The term "alpha" in the investment world refers to the amount of "excess risk-adjusted return" relative to expected market returns. The financial giant Vanguard completed a study[14] in which they attempted to quantify the amount of alpha that a professional advisor might deliver in different categories. In all, they determined that the range of potential value that can be added through working with an advisor is as high as 3% per year. (A link to the study is in Appendix C.)

Of the total amount of alpha that a good financial advisor can provide, the bulk is centered on three categories. In order of importance:

1. **Behavioral Coaching**, which is helping you make good, informed decisions through market cycles.

2. **Spending Strategy**, which means working to make certain that distributions are efficiently made from accounts

---

14   Vanguard: https://advisors.vanguard.com/insights/article/putting-a-value-o n-your-value-quantifying-advisors-alpha

with different tax treatments.

3. **Asset Allocation**, which refers to diversification among asset classes and strategic, periodic rebalancing.

Shopping for a financial professional can be overwhelming, given the endless list of industry job titles and alphabet soup of credentials. When shopping for financial advice, it's good to keep your individual goals in mind and then interview professionals who have the experience and focus that best suit your needs.

Below is a list of professional designations and their meanings to help you search for the professional best for you.

<u>**New Investor**</u>: Designations geared toward people who are new or newer to investing.

- ➤ AAMS (Accredited Asset Management Specialist)
- ➤ ABFP (Accredited Behavioral Finance Professional)
- ➤ CRPC (Chartered Retirement Planning Counselor)
- ➤ FPQP (Financial Paraplanner Qualified Professional)
- ➤ RLP (Registered Life Planner)
- ➤ WMCP (Wealth Management Certified Professional)

<u>**Core Investor**</u>: Designations designed to serve investors who have a moderate level of investment experience.

- ➤ ABFP (Accredited Behavioral Finance Professional)
- ➤ CFP (Certified Financial Planner)
- ➤ ChFC (Chartered Financial Consultant)
- ➤ CIMA (Certified Investment Management Analyst)

<u>High Net Worth/Ultra High Net Worth Investor:</u> Designations geared toward people with high net worth.

- ➤ CAP (Chartered Advisor in Philanthropy)
- ➤ CPWA (Certified Private Wealth Advisor)
- ➤ CWS (Certified Wealth Strategist)

<u>Niche Designation Segments:</u> Designations geared toward clients with specific investment needs such as business exit strategies, company retirement plans, life insurance underwriting needs, etc.

- ➤ ADPA (Accredited Domestic Partnership Advisor)
- ➤ CEPA (Certified Exit Planning Advisor)
- ➤ CKA (Certified Kingdom Advisor)
- ➤ CLU (Chartered Life Underwriter)
- ➤ CSRIC (Chartered SRI Counselor)
- ➤ CRPC (Chartered Retirement Plan Specialist)
- ➤ RICP (Retirement Income Certified Professional)

APPENDIX B: Budgeting: Categories and Concepts

Be prepared to share your monthly and annual expenses in today's dollars with your financial advisor. They include:

<u>Housing and Taxes</u>

- ➤ Rent or mortgage
- ➤ Federal, state, local taxes
- ➤ Property taxes

> ➤ Repairs and maintenance

Note about inflation: If you have a mortgage on your residence and the monthly payment includes escrow for property taxes and home insurance, *it can make a significant impact to break out principal and interest separately from those items.* While almost everything else in your life is subject to inflation, principal and interest on a fixed rate mortgage will always be the same. Moreover, there will be a point in your life when the mortgage may be paid off completely, and this significant expense might fall off your required spending.

<u>Utilities</u>

> ➤ Gas

> ➤ Electric

> ➤ Water and sewer

> ➤ Trash and recycling

> ➤ TV (and all subscription services)

> ➤ Internet

<u>Insurance</u>

> ➤ Auto

> ➤ Health, dental, vision

> ➤ Disability

> ➤ Life insurance

> ➤ Long-term care

<u>Retirement Savings</u>

> ➤ Taxable

- Pre-tax (401k, SEP, Simple, 403b)
- After-tax (Roth k, Roth IRA)
- Health Savings Account (HSA)

<u>Loans</u>

- Auto loan or lease
- Student loans
- Home equity
- Consumer debt
- Other
  - Business loans
  - Real estate investment loans

<u>Other Expenses</u>

- Clothing
- Gifts
  - Birthday and holiday spending
  - Kids/Grandkids 529 plans or UTMA (Unified Transfers to Minors Act) accounts
- Memberships, subscriptions, and dues
- Personal items
- Transportation
  - Tolls
  - Public transportation
  - Fuel

- o   Parking

<u>Miscellaneous</u>

- ➤   Charitable contributions

- ➤   Memberships, subscriptions, and dues

- ➤   Entertainment

  - o   Dining out

  - o   Travel

  - o   Hobbies

<u>Other Obligations</u>

- ➤   Alimony

- ➤   Childcare

  - o   Lessons

  - o   Sports

APPENDIX C: Resources, Research, Partnerships, and Notes

Below is a list of a few websites I've discovered that could be helpful to you in building your playbook. Note that not all of these are businesses or organizations that I have used personally. I cannot vouch for each of them 100% yet.

You can find a living, evolving list of resources and partnerships like these at my publishing website, <u>www.illuminare-press.com.</u>

I welcome your reviews or other recommendations! You might just contribute something that will help evolve the list

and help others that are creating their own Second Half plans!

Check out these resources related to legacy topics.

www.storyworth.com

www.legalzoom.com

www.trustandwill.com

Check out these resources related to volunteer topics.

www.volunteermatch.org

Men's Shed Association – Shoulder to Shoulder (usmenssheds.org)

Check out these resources related to connections to all your people.

www.ancestry.com

https://www.health.harvard.edu/mind-and-mood/the-power-of-forgiveness

Check out these resources related to places to visit and recording your wins.

www.Tauck.com

www.costcotravel.com

www.holycowcanvas.com

www.conquestmaps.com

www.pushpintravelmaps.com

Sometimes, a good search engine can be your best friend! Search the internet for any type of activity near where you live. Here's a brain dump of ideas to get you started:

Running, race car driving, hiking trails, writing class, baking class, home repair instruction, wine making, beer brewing, bourbon tasting, kickboxing, yoga, zip lining, axe throwing, archery, paddleboard, scuba diving, rollerblading, surfing, roller coasters, sky diving, water skiing, snow skiing, rafting, canoeing, helicopter rides, hot air balloon rides, bike trails, off-road adventures, snowmobiling, cave exploration, horse riding, dune buggies, small plane rides, waterfall tours, shooting ranges, archery, duck hunting, fishing, golf, paintball, tennis, pickleball, tennis, racquetball, softball, baseball, soccer, disk golf, sailing, snorkeling, camping, wine tasting, boating, ice skating, concerts, theater, music lessons, watercolor classes, chess clubs, bible study, dance lessons, line dancing, singing lessons, calligraphy lessons, genealogy research, ballet performances, CrossFit gyms, cooking classes, meditation groups, garden clubs, book clubs, dog training, foraging groups, meditation, weaving classes, pottery classes, song writing, storm chasing, coin collecting, polar bear plunges, time capsules, bowling, kite flying, barbeque instruction, sewing, knitting, woodworking, community theater, glass blowing, website design, origami or scrapbooking.

About the Author

Ed McClellan, CFP, CEPA, AAMS, is the senior partner of a wealth management team in Ann Arbor, Michigan. He graduated with honors in sociology from Western Michigan University in 1983 and obtained his MBA from the University of Michigan in 2005. Ed leads a team that includes an associate financial advisor and two extremely valuable office administrators, who work very hard to keep him (and their clients) organized and efficient. Ed's been married for more than 40 years to his wife, Karen. Together and separately, they continue to work on their own Second Half playbooks. They are very proud to have two fully launched, happily married daughters and four practically perfect grandchildren.